# Teach Your Dog

# Italian

Funny & surprisingly clever books. Love. Love.
*DAWN FRENCH, ACTOR & COMEDIAN*

Anne Cakebread not only has the best
name in the Universe, she has also come
up with a brilliantly fun book which will help
humans and canines learn new languages.
*RICHARD HERRING, COMEDIAN*

I'm fed up with teaching my dogs all these
different languages. It's like the Tower of Babel
in here.
*LUCY GANNON, WRITER*

People are crackers, mate. They think you can
teach dogs Italian, when we all know they only
speak French.
*ARTHUR SMITH, WRITER & COMEDIAN*

# Teach Your Dog

# ITALIAN

Anne Cakebread

Thank you to:
Helen, Marcie, Lily and Nina,
my family, friends and neighbours in
St Dogmaels for all their support and
encouragement, Camillo Gatta and
Carolyn at Y Lolfa for Italian translations
and pronunciations.
Grazie.

In memory of Frieda, who started us on
the *Teach Your Dog* journey.

*First impression: 2022*

© Anne Cakebread & Y Lolfa Cyf., 2022

Illustrations and design by Anne Cakebread

ISBN: 978-1-912631-40-7

Published and printed in Wales on paper from well-maintained forests by
Y Lolfa Cyf., Talybont, Ceredigion SY24 5HE
*e-mail* ylolfa@ylolfa.com
*website* www.ylolfa.com
*tel* 01970 832 304
*fax* 832 782

*I grew up only speaking English.*
*When I moved to west Wales, I adopted Frieda,*
*a rescue whippet, who would only obey*
*Welsh commands.*
*Slowly, whilst dealing with Frieda, I realised that I was*
*overcoming my nerves about speaking Welsh aloud,*
*and my Welsh was improving as a result*
*– this gave me the idea of creating a series of books*
*to help others learn.*
*You don't even have to go abroad to practise.*
*If you haven't got a dog, any pet or soft toy will do:*
*just have fun learning and speaking a new language.*

*– Anne Cakebread*

"Hello"

**"Ciao"**

*pron:*
**"Chow"**

"Come here"

"Vieni qui"

pron:

"Vee-<u>any</u> kwee"

stress
this

"Stop!"

"Stai fermo♂/
ferma♀!"

pron:

"Sty fair-mo♂/fair-ma♀!"

'o'
as in
'hot'

'a'
as in
'man'

roll the
'r'
slightly

roll the
'r'
slightly

"Do you want a cuddle?"

# "Vuoi le coccole?"

*pron:*

***"Vwoy***
***le kok-o-le?"***

*'e' as in 'met'*

*stress this*

*'o' as in 'hot'*

*'e' as in 'met'*

"Fetch!"

# "Vai a prenderla!"

*pron:*

## "Vye <u>a</u> <u>pren</u>-dare-l<u>a</u>!"

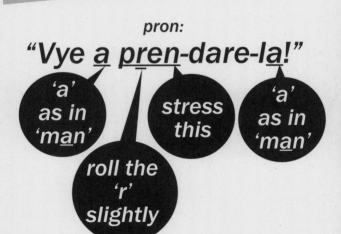

'a' as in 'm<u>a</u>n'

roll the 'r' slightly

stress this

'a' as in 'm<u>a</u>n'

"Leave it!"

**"Lasciala!"**

*pron:*
**"Lasha-la!"**

'a'
as in
'man'

"Sit"

"**Siediti**"

*pron:*
*"See-edit-ee"*

"No!"

"No!"

*pron:*
"N**o**!"

'o'
as in
'h**o**t'

"Stay!"

## "Non ti muovere!"

pron:

"Non tee mwov-<u>e</u>-<u>re</u>!"

'e' as in 'm<u>e</u>t'

'e' as in 'm<u>e</u>t'

roll the 'r' slightly

"Bathtime"

# "Ora di fare il bagno"

roll the 'r' slightly

pron:

## "Au_r_a dee fah-_re_ ill ban-y_o_"

'e' as in 'm_e_t'

'o' as in 'h_o_t'

"Bedtime"

## "Ora di andare a letto"

roll the 'r' slightly

'e' as in 'met'

pron:

"Aura dee ann-dah-re a let-o"

'a' as in 'man'

hold the 't'

'o' as in 'hot'

"Lunchtime"

# "Ora di pranzo"

pron:

## "Au_ra dee p_ran-z_o"

roll
the 'r'
slightly

'o'
as in
'ho_t'

“Are you full?”

# “Sei pieno / piena ?”

*pron:*

**“Say pee-air-no / pee-air-na ?”**

stress this

stress this

‘a’ as in ‘man’

‘o’ as in ‘hot’

"All gone"

"È tutto finito"

pron:

*"Ey toot-o fin-eeto"*

hold
the
't'

'o'
as in
'hot'

"Good morning"

## "Buongiorno"

*pron:*

**"Bwon-jor-no"**

roll the 'r' slightly

'o' as in 'hot'

"Goodnight"

## "Buonanotte"

*pron:*

## "Bwon-<u>a</u>-no<u>t</u>-<u>e</u>"

'a'
as in
'm<u>a</u>n'

'e'
as in
'm<u>e</u>t'

hold
the
't'

"Don't scratch!"

"Non grattarti!"

pron:
"Non grat-arty!"

roll the 'r' slightly

hold the 't'

roll the 'r' slightly

"Let's go..."

"**Andiamo...**"

pron:

"*Andy-ah-mo...*"

'o'
as in
'h<u>o</u>t'

"Go down"

"Scendi giù"

pron:
"Shen-dee joo"

stress
this

"Up you go"

"Sali"

pron:
"*Sah-lee*"

stress
this

"Go straight ahead"

"Vai dritto"

pron:

"Vye drit-o"

roll the 'r' slightly

'o' as in 'hot'

hold the 't'

"Go left"

## "Vai a sinistra"

pron:

## "Vye a sin-ee-stra"

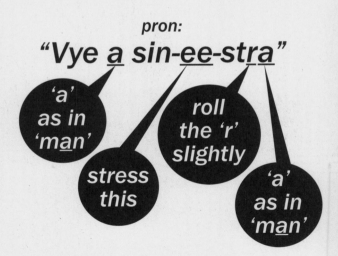

'a' as in 'man'

stress this

roll the 'r' slightly

'a' as in 'man'

"Turn left"

# "Gira a sinistra"

'a' as in 'man'

pron:

'a' as in 'man'

"Jeera a sin-ee-stra"

roll the 'r' slightly

stress this

roll the 'r' slightly

“How’s it going?”

# “Come va?”

*pron:*

***“Kom-e va?”***

*‘e’ as in ‘met’*

*‘a’ as in ‘man’*

"Do you
want to play?"

"Vuoi giocare?"

pron:

"Vwoy jock-ah-_re_?"

roll
the 'r'
slightly

'e'
as in
'm_e_t'

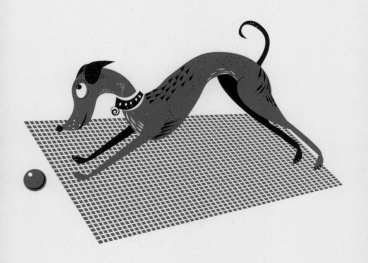

"Lie down"

"Sdraiati"

pron:
"Z*d*r*y*-*a*-tee"

roll
the 'r'
slightly

'a'
as in
'm*a*n'

"Say 'please'!"

"Di' 'per favore'!"

*pron:*
"Dee 'pai_r_ f_a_-vor-_e_'!"

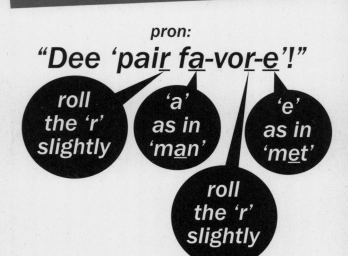

roll
the 'r'
slightly

'a'
as in
'm_a_n'

'e'
as in
'm_e_t'

roll
the 'r'
slightly

"Can I have the ball?"

"Mi dai la palla?"

pron:

"Me die la pal-a?"

'a' as in 'man'

hold the 'l'

"Can I have some red wine?"

"Mi dai del vino rosso?"

pron:

"Me die dell veeno ross-o?"

'o' as in 'hot'

roll the 'r' slightly

hold the 'ss'

'o' as in 'hot'

# "Well done!"

**"Bravo!"** 🧍‍♂️ / **"Brava!"** 🧍‍♀️

"It's warm"

## "Fa caldo"

pron:

### "Fa cal-do"

'a'
as in
'man'

'o'
as in
'hot'

"What nice weather!"

## "Che bel tempo!"

*pron:*
## *"Kay bell tem-po!"*

'o'
as in
'hot'

"It's raining"

"Piove"

pron:
"Pee-or-ve"

'e'
as in
'met'

“Are you happy?”

**“Sei contento / contenta ?”**

*pron:*

“Say con-tent-o / con-tent-a ?”

‘o’ as in ‘hot’

‘a’ as in ‘man’

"Who's snoring?"

## "Chi russa?"

*pron:*

## "Key <u>roo</u>-<u>sa</u>?"

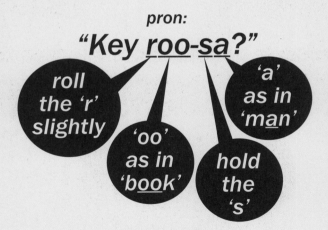

roll the 'r' slightly

'oo' as in '<u>boo</u>k'

hold the 's'

'a' as in '<u>ma</u>n'

"Have you got enough room?"

"Hai abbastanza spazio?"

*pron:*

"*Eye abba-stantsa spats-yo?*"

'o' as in 'hot'

'a' as in 'man'

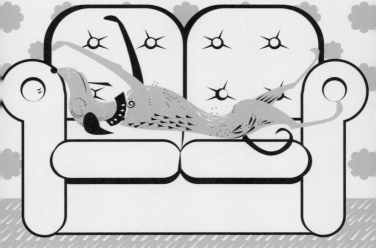

"See you soon"

"A tra poco"

*pron:*

"A tra pock-o"

'A'
as in
'man'

'o'
as in
'hot'

"Be quiet!"

"Silenzio!"

pron:
"See-Lent-seeyo!"

'o'
as in
'hot'

“Who did that?”

**“Chi è stato / stata ?”**

*pron:*

***“Key ey start-o / start-a ?”***

*‘o’ as in ‘hot’*

*‘a’ as in ‘man’*

"There's a queue for the loo"

**"C'è la fila per il bagno"**

'a' as in 'm<u>a</u>n'

pron:

**"Chay l<u>a</u> feel<u>a</u> pai<u>r</u> ill ban-y<u>o</u>"**

roll the 'r' slightly

'o' as in 'h<u>o</u>t'

## 1

**"uno"**

*pron:*

**"oo-n<u>o</u>"**

'o'
as in
'h<u>o</u>t'

## 2

**"due"**

*pron:*

**"doo-<u>e</u>"**

'e'
as in
'm<u>e</u>t'

3

## "tre"

*pron:*

## "tr<u>e</u>"

'e'
as in
'm<u>e</u>t'

4

## "quattro"

*pron:*

## "kwat-r<u>o</u>"

'o'
as in
'h<u>o</u>t'

9

"**nove**"

*pron:*

"**norv-e̱**"

'e'
as in
'me̱t'

**10**

**"dieci"**

*pron:*

**"dee-air-chee"**

"Thank you"

## "Grazie"

pron:

## "Graht-see-yeh"

roll
the 'r'
slightly

"Merry Christmas"

"Buon Natale"

pron:

"Bwon Nat-ah-le̲"

'e'
as in
'me̲t'

"Congratulations!"

"Congratulazioni!"

*pron:*
"Con**gra**-too-**la**tsee-orny!"

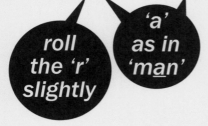

roll the 'r' slightly

'a' as in 'm**a**n'

"Happy Birthday"

## "Tanti auguri"

*pron:*

*"Tanty ow-goo-ree"*

stress
this

roll
the 'r'
slightly

"I love you"

## "Ti voglio bene"

pron:

## "Tee voll-yo bear-ne"

'o'
as in
'hot'

'e'
as in
'met'

"Goodbye"

"Ciao"

*pron:*
**"Chow"**